A Passage

by

Jemimah Ngu

To Tabatha,
One of the greatest friends and people the world has ever seen. I can't wait to see where your art takes you.

Copyright © 2019 Jemimah Ngu

All rights reserved, including the right to reproduce this book, or portions thereof in any form. No part of this text may be reproduced, transmitted, downloaded, decompiled, reverse engineered, or stored, in any form or introduced into any information storage and retrieval system, in any form or by any means, whether electronic or mechanical without the express written permission of the author.

ISBN: 978-0-244-50568-4

Dedicated to the Lord God Almighty, who gave me this gift, and to all those who speak through their poetry.

Foreword

A Passage of Time is a collection of poems composed and written by Jemimah Ngu with deep reflection on some existential realities of human life. A critical look at the poems shows the different stages of her reflections in relationship with the proportionality of her rational ability, age and experience in human society.

Her maiden group of poems clearly illustrate a curious young mind exploring the beauty of nature as a blessing of God to humanity. The second group of her poems shows the thinking of a girl that appreciates family bond with associated responsibility of each member of a family. In the third category of her poems, she basically focuses her contemplation on the concerns, worries and wishes of a girl that is maturing to understand the differences that exist between a male and a female child; and the need for adequate protection of children, especially the girl child. The subsequent group of her poems is actually a true reflection of a girl that has attained the consciousness of love, hate and the need to be proud of her personality, differences and background. This group of her poems underlines the social responsibilities and experiences of life as a young child given the opportunity to explore her immediate neighbourhood and wider society. The last category of her poems is full of gratitude and admiration of her parents for the socio-cultural values already inculcated in her so as to live responsibly with others in the society.

The common impression that is evident in all these poems is that Jemimah is a new star in the world of poetry that will become brighter and brighter with age and time. If she is encouraged and promoted by those who will appreciate her little beginning, she will soon be known all over the world like J.P. Clark, Chinua Achebe, Gabriel Okara, Niyi Osundare and Wole Soyinka of Nigeria; Anta David Diop and Leopold Senghor of Senegal; Mbella Sonne Dipoko, Patrice Kayo and Patrice Nganang of Cameroon and other great poets in Africa and all over the world.

Rev. Fr. Dr. Aso Williams
Seminary of All Saints,
Edo State, Nigeria

Acknowledgements

I would like to thank my parents: Dr (Mrs) Pascaline Ngu and Dr Jude (Teddy) Ngu for encouraging me to compile my poems into a book and ensuring it is published. They along with my brother Samuel Ngu provided moral support and love for my writing – and for that I thank them.

The spark igniting the zeal to publish my work first came from St Cloud Elementary School in West Orange, New Jersey, USA. I have reproduced that early poem, *Snowflake*, here. St Cloud encouraged many of us to submit work for consideration, I never thought my work would scale through, it did and that zeal to publish was instilled in me.

I also want to thank Dr. (Mrs) Mercy Tembon, Mrs. Linda Alvarez, Mr. Richard Boden and Miss Noemi Garcia; all of whom took the time to read my work and give a review.

Reverend (Dr) Father Aso Williams was most generous with his time and reviewed and wrote a foreword at short notice – Padre I thank you too.

Table of Contents

1. My First Published Poem
   - Snowflake..1
2. Double-Digit Era
   - What Are Dreams?......................................2
   - Mothers and Fathers...................................3
   - Rainbows..4
   - The Market Life.....................................5-6
   - The Only One..7
   - Popularity..8
   - The World of Fear......................................9
   - Chores..10
   - Happiness Brings Smiles...........................11
   - Study Time...12
   - What Are Cousins For?..............................13
   - Computers..14
   - Vegetables...15
   - Week(ly) Names.......................................16

- Who Are True Friends?...........................17
- Rice...18
- The Creation Story (Jemimah's Version)......................................19
- Money vs Honey...20
- Mosquitos......................................21
- The Definition of Love...22
- I am Nine.......................................23
- Faith...24
- Famous...25
- My School Teachers.......................................26

3. Pre-Teen Era

- Alice in Wonderland......................................27
- A Poem for Mothers..28
- Who I Am......................................29
- Writing..30
- School...31

4. Teen Era

- The Haters......................................32
- These Days....................................33-34
- Naira vs Dollar................................35

viii

- Nigeria's Recurring Nightmare: The Fuel Crisis...36-37
- Too Many People..38-39
- Love Girls, Don't Hate Them...40
- The Tie..41
- Good Enough...42
- Enemies..43
- Who Am I?...44-45
- The Witch...46
- The Dragon...47

5. The Sixteen Era

- What I See..48
- My Mother's Eyes...49
- July 6th...50-51

x

My First Published Poem

Snowflake

S is for children singing Christmas carols
N is for nutcrackers
O is for outside playing with friends
W is for winter
F is for falling snowflakes
L is for laughing all day long
A is for ashes through my tears
K is for keeping warm
E is for everyone loves snow

Note:
This poem was first published in the anthology of poems in: **Creative Communication.** *Snowflake.* [ed.] Thomas Worthen. *A Celebration of Poets, East, Grades 4-12, Summer 2011.* Smithfield : Creative Communication, 2011, p. 162.

Double-Digit Era

What Are Dreams?

Dreams are more than imagination
They are peaceful thoughts
Dreams are stronger than nightmares
They are miracles in your brain
Dreams are our future
They are more than we expect them to be
Dreams are like mysteries we are waiting to solve
Dreams are lovely things

Mothers and Fathers

Mothers work very hard
Fathers are strong and brave
Mothers will protect us from harm
Fathers keep the boys away
Mothers make girls look divine
Fathers are handsome and nice
Mothers are pretty and sweet
But there is just one thing
They both love us

Rainbows

Rainbows come after the rain
Rainbows have seven colours
Rainbows are bright like the blazing sun
Rainbows amaze the eyes of young children
Rainbows are worth more than a pot of gold
Rainbows are slides full of colourful beams
Rainbows are like peaceful dreams
Rainbows are amazing

The Market Life

It's filthy,
But full of determined people
It's stinky,
But the people like to sell goods
It's not ShopRite,
But it has reasonable prices
It's like a huge kitchen,
With a lot of tools
These people all do this to survive,
Like the rest of us
This is how they live.
This is the market life.

Context:

In Nigeria, along with most African countries, there are open markets. In these markets you can buy food, clothes, shoes, and make-up. Very many different products are sold.

In Nigeria there are gutters, which are filled to the brim with dirty water and other rubbish. The hard-working traders of the market are not put off by the smell of these gutters. They have an aim, and that is to sell. They use their wits and their common sense to make a living, and for that I respect them.

ShopRite Supermarkets across Nigeria – are part of South Africa's Shoprite Holdings. They operate almost 3,000 outlets in 15 countries across Africa.

The Only One

Being an only child is a cold, lonely place
It's like a dark hole caving in on you
Lonely is the meaning of an only child

I wish I had some siblings
Although, I do have my parents
So I don't feel lonely after all

Context:
I wrote this prior to my mother giving birth to my lovely
brother Samuel eleven years after I was born. For so long
I had wanted a sibling. I am grateful to have Sam in my
life. No longer am I the only one, thank God.

Popularity

What is the popular side of life?
It doesn't matter who knows you or likes you
It matters for your character

Are you nice and sweet, like sugar?
Or are you mean and sour, like bullies?
You should be nice and sweet, like sugar

Be like this and I bet that,
You'll be an angel when you go to heaven
Do not break the commandments or commit a sin
Do what's right to show the popular side of life
Be good, not bad

The World of Fear

What frightens all of us is not the dark
It isn't lions, tigers, or thunder
It is the nightmares we think will come true

Why is this what frightens us?
Who knows why, even?

But it's OK
This is the only scary thing in the world
Although we can stop that
With the magical power of dreams
                    Dreams vs Nightmares

Chores

Clean the dishes
Mop the floor
Oh, my goodness, what a bore!
Do this
Do that
I'd rather not
There's so much to do
Can't I get a break?
It seems like forever
But the good thing is I get paid

Happiness Brings Smiles

What is happiness?
It is the magic that brings smiles to the world
Smiles bring joy all around
Joy brings good people to the town
Good people make a healthy city
A healthy city makes awesome states and countries
Awesome states and countries,
Make the whole world go round
But it all starts, with a beaming glow of happiness

Study Time

Oh no, it's study time
I have to study now
I'd rather smell the stink of a skunk
It will make me smart
But I don't want to study
                    Boo work

What are Cousins For?

When your sister's in Las Vegas
And your brother's in New York
Cousins are great to have around,
When you think you'll be your parents' BFF
They'll play with you until it's time for bed
Cousins are good to have around
                    Go, Cousins

Computers

Typing every day
Typing every night
The computer is the best invention in sight
I love to go on it
It is really amazing
I love the computer

Vegetables

Veggies are very good for you
Broccoli, spinach, and cabbage
They are all crops

Some people love them
But I certainly do not
They are gross in all ways
I may vomit for days

I get why God made the earth and the stars
But why on earth did he say
"Let there be vegetables"

Week(ly) Names

Monday, Tuesday, Wednesday, Thursday, Friday,
Saturday, and Sunday

Are these really names?
Hello, Monday
Hello, Sunday

I'm so confused

What is up with these names?
They are surely playing games
Because they couldn't really be names

Who Are True Friends?

True friends are the people who don't laugh at you,
But who laugh with you
They are the ones who care for you
They love you for who you are
They are the ones who have got your back at all times
If not for true friends what would there be in life?

True friends are with us till the end
Oh, how it's lovely to have
True friends

Rice

Rice is nice
Rice doesn't give you lice
But the side effects from eating too much rice

Are the following:
Rice crazy
Too lazy

Maybe lice
Not so nice

Now do you like
Rice?

The Creation Story (Jemimah's Version)

1. God said, "Let there be Sprite," and there was Sprite.
2. God said, "Let there be cement," and there was cement.
3. God said, "Let there be weaves (for your hair)," and there were weaves.
4. God said, "Let there be nuns," and there were nuns.
5. God said, "Let there be bleach," and there was bleach.
6. God said, "Let there be ham," and there was ham.
7. God rested. And the rest of us were tested … on the story of the Creation.

Money vs Honey

I need some money
I need some honey
I need money to buy honey
I love honey and money but I really can't decide
Money vs Honey …
Now I know what to do

Eeny meeny miny money
Go and catch the beautiful honey

Money, honey, honey, money
Oh, sweetheart, I really need some money

Mosquitos

I completely dislike mosquitos
They don't even taste like Fritos

They will bite with all their might,
And they will fight for your blood

Mosquitos are very irritating
So much that I almost feel like fainting

Mosquitos are ugly paintings on a broken wall

Soon one day those paintings will fall
And never again, will there be
Any mosquitos, that don't taste like Fritos

The Definition of Love

The definition of love
Is greater than the sky above
It is like flying with doves
I love to love all those around
I feel so free

Loving is a wonderful thing
I think that no one can truly define love, but
It is a wonderful thing

I Am Nine

Hello,
I am nine.
It's a fact that the world is mine
I am like the stars that shine
Truly, I am divine
You cannot hurt me
Even if you try
I am not that easy to break, like a fly
And you ask, "Why?"
It's because I am nine

Faith

Your faith is a state of grace
It's as beautiful as your smiling face
Faith helps you to submit yourself to God
It is what leads you to peace and prosperity

If faith wasn't in the world,
We would fail to do many things

So have faith and you'll never regret it

Famous

If you want to be famous
You have to be gracious
It's not about you
It's about us, the audience

You'll have ups and downs, but
Don't wear a frown
It will make you look like a sad clown
So when you have good qualities
And you're extremely gracious
Now you know that you are famous

My School Teachers

Our teachers teach us
Everything we need to know that day

They will go to mass and while they pray, they'll say
Dear Lord, I hope my teaching skills will pay
For all the students I've taught today
Amen

Thank God for our teachers and for our principal too
If not for them
There would be nothing to do

We love you

Pre-teen Era

Alice in Wonderland

Alice in Wonderland;
A land like no other
Found in the imagination
Full of folk tales and riddles

And later, you realise it was all just a dream
After, waking up and trying to find your way home

A Poem for Mothers

My, oh my, what a beautiful mother I have
Oh, God is so smart to grant me such a blessing
This mother of mine shall continue to grow, on the
Lord's vine
Happiness is what I see when I look at her
Extraordinary love to everyone
Right there to lend a helping hand

Happy Mother's Day

Who I Am

Jolly at the right time
Energetic 24/7
Me when I need to be and want to be
I love my life
Marvellous at special things
Acquiring changes that I want and need
Heaven is what I want the most

Writing

I write what I feel
I write what I think
I write what appeals to me
I write what I want
I write what I say
I write forever until my hand stops writing

School

Success from now and into the future
Cool … sometimes
Hurts to go but it's for the best
Opportunities to learn and to grow
Out of this world
Lovin' it

Teen Era

The Haters

They hate the way I walk
The way I dress
The way I talk
They look at me with disgust
Like I'm dirt, or metal with rust

They hate on me,
Because they envy me
I am true to myself
If you don't like it, I don't care

They hate the way I look,
Some hate the colour of my skin
But I am beautiful as can be,
Because I know God created me

I don't hate the haters,
The haters hate on me
But I ignore the haters
Because when I do, I get the victory

These Days

These days there's dirty water and no light
You have to get a bucket and a bright torchlight
Every day you see a rat, a lizard, or a roach
Those nasty, pesky creatures that I don't like to approach

Some pee in the grass
Some eat from the trash
Some are so blessed
They eat three meals a day
No more, no less

The outside is beautiful, the trees and the breeze
It makes you feel somewhat free
The blazing sun's rays make you feel superhot
And turn you black like the charcoal you use
For your cooking pot

It might not be America, but in many ways it's better
In Africa I got a tough skin and expanded my brain
I learnt how to use street sense without stress or strain

My Africa is quite nice and I want you to know that
It's got culture and substance,
And that's a fact.
Please don't look down on Africa;
But give her, her deserving praise
For she has done much for this world in so many ways

Context:
I had the opportunity of living in Nigeria for six years as well as travelling to other African countries like Rwanda, Kenya, and the Republic of Benin. I've explored these countries and want my readers to know that the news doesn't show you enough of the beauty that is the continent of Africa. Take a trip to any country there and you'll be amazed when you find yourself wanting to stay.

Naira vs Dollar

One US Dollar to 350 Naira … This is insane

The naira is like a bronze medal while the dollar is gold
It seems that it'll stay that way,
Even when Nigeria is 100 years old

The leader won't let naira or dollars leave the country
And even the citizens,
Have their flights cancelled or delayed
Even with their costly flight tickets already paid
No summer or winter or Easter vacation
For him or the entire nation

It's true, the naira has lost its value
And that's just the cold hard truth
But keep your hopes up for the future, dear friends
For the rate must surely go down soon

Context:

The Naira is Nigeria's national currency. It is a weak
currency and continuously fluctuates against the US
Dollar. The most painful thing about this is that one naira
used to equal one US dollar. It is now very expensive to
import goods so therefore basic goods and services are
expensive, and people who have small incomes struggle
to feed their families.

Nigeria's Recurring Nightmare: The Fuel Crisis

What does everybody want? Fuel
What does everybody need? Fuel

Whether this is a problem of scarcity or hoarding
The people are hungry for what keeps them going

This crisis is bad
And keeps getting worse
The fuel lines are long
Like the lines at a sale

It never reduces
But only increases
When will it end
When will it stop?
My mind could just go pop

In our daily lives we use transportation
Car, buses, trucks, and planes
They're all the same

Fuel gives them energy
The way sleep gives us a boost

I think we can all agree that
This is a nightmare
So someone should stop this,
We have no time to spare

Context:
In Nigeria most people have private cars and drivers or use public transport, which means that fuel is a basic necessity. There are periods in the year where there is fuel scarcity, especially around Christmas. And for a nation dependent on fuel that's not good.

Too Many People

We can't breathe
There's no space
More and more people all over the place

Such is Lagos Life
It's like Africa's own New York,
Guess that's why it's so famous

We wake up to traffic, poverty, and unemployment
Because we are too many in number

Leaving some people with no jobs
And no money
The people off to work are always stuck in traffic
And bombarded by those who beg

Other states don't have such a large population
So why not go there instead?
Why make the overcrowding spread?
Do you want to join those who don't have a bed?
Or those who beg?
Or those with no jobs, money or roofs over their heads?

Context:

Lagos is like the 'New York' of Nigeria. Trust me when I say that Lagos never sleeps. It is filled with people to the brim and its population keeps growing. When people move to Nigeria they choose to live in either Lagos or Abuja, and most people go for Lagos. On the streets of Lagos, many poor people stand on the road and tap car windows, begging for money. It's hard to drive away especially when stuck in traffic.

Love Girls, Don't Hate Them

Who are girls?
They are beautiful creatures, moulded by God's hands
And they should be treated like the queens that they are

Some heartless men with the dirtiest minds
Treat them like objects most of the time
They tear off their clothes and do what they please
They silence their cries and screams with ease

And what happens when these criminals get caught?
The judges take their side,
Whether they've been bribed or not

After such a trauma,
It seems scary to speak out
They cry on the inside,
When they just want to shout

So please help us fight,
Stand tall and proud
And defend our girls,
Say it bold and loud

The Tie

We were younger,
Then we got older
Smarter, stronger, faster, bolder

All they did was give us a tie
And what I thought I knew, was a lie

Friends became my frenemies
Enemies were sometimes friends
People who seemed to be close to me
Were further away than I thought

Tears, tears, and more tears

It's painful how one little thing
Can destroy something huge

The tie should not have been given to us
It does more damage;

Take it back;

School should go back to the way it was

Good Enough

Am I self-conscious? Yes
Do I like attention? Sometimes
Compliments? Of course
But I still feel, I'm not good enough

Being a teen is hard,
In these times it's so tough
Can never tell if you're good enough

Caring too much about yourself in others' eyes
Because in yours there's too much to despise

If the boys will like me
If the girls will befriend me
And why do I have so many enemies?

But I've learnt that I must learn to love myself
It took some time, but I've got better

Sometimes overthinking has
Brought my self-esteem down
But I push through and pick myself up from the ground
I've come to know that regardless of
How I'm seen in the eyes of others
Lo and behold,
      I am good enough

Enemies

Don't hate me because I am beautiful
Don't mock me because I am blessed
Don't gossip about me because I am loved
And don't spit at my feet because
I choose not to be stressed

Talk … oh, keep talking,
It won't hurt me,
I will keep on flaunting my bouncing personality

It's funny how you think I care
If I did,
It wouldn't be fair,
You'd have the last laugh instead of me
Which means I'd have no victory

You think I'm scared?
Try me
You're what?
A bear…

I'm a lioness,
A queen
These people I call my enemies
Ain't got nothing on me

Who Am I?

I am a girl who is sad inside,
But no one knows
I plaster on a smile all day just for show

I am a girl with big dreams
That I feel are not supported
So I had to find something else to dream about
Just to satisfy them

I am a girl who fears her future
A girl with people who say they're her friends
But, who replace her when she leaves
A girl struggling to believe in herself

I am a girl who longs to be something
Amazing
Incredible
Extraordinary
A girl who does not want to let everyone down

A girl who would like it
If a guy complimented her on her looks for once
Who thought she was not just pretty,
But also beautiful

A girl who doesn't just want
But needs
Somebody to listen to her, and
Let her cry and whine and to comfort her
I am this girl

The Witch

When you first took up your new role
You were an innocent soul
But as the years went by
That good, pure lady said bye-bye

No more a nice lady but a witch
With her evil cackle and constant eye twitch

To go out of the house is a problem
It's to go to school and to church and that's the end

I need to put a bell on you,
With all the times you peep in my room
When you buy me snacks, it lasts just for a day
No wonder I'm the girl who's always hungry

So Mummy, I love you
Really I do
But you're not just my mummy
You're a witch too

The Dragon

You see, almost every mother is a witch
In the mind of their child
But not every mother is a dragon

My mother is the only mother who is a dragon

She doesn't breathe fire but there are flames in her eyes
She wears the face of an innocent woman as a disguise

I can seldom have juice, but I can always have water
It is a struggle being her daughter

When I want something she says,
What have you done for me today?
Na wa o
Just say yes or no, and I'll be on my way

You see, the struggle is very real
I just don't understand *what* is her deal

The Sixteen Era

What I See

I've seen heart,
I've seen sweat,
I've seen tears,
I've seen smiling faces and ringing ears
I've seen girls who went from juniors to seniors,
I've seen girls who are not inferior but superior.

I see girls who will never conform
I see girls who will take the world by storm
I see six years of memories in your eyes
I see great heights and clear skies

I'll see dominators, conquerors, and queen bees,
I'll see PhDs, second-class uppers and first-class degrees
I'll see excellent mothers, mentors, and wives,
I'll see women who will do nothing less than change
lives

My Mother's Eyes

Her eyes pierce deep in your soul,
They have a strong effect even when they're closed
Those eyes move north, south, east, and west
They can see you when you're naughty, and when you're
at your best

Those eyes, they light up with fire
They scare you and haunt you and make you perspire
Wherever you are, they will find you
How they found you
There's no clue

If in public you'll behave your best
In somebody's house you're never a guest
You want to rest, But you see the eyes in your dreams
And you try and try, But there's no escape
It seems

Beware, beware, the eyes are here
Her eyes are far, and they are near
So don't slip up,
Because I fear
Those horrid eyes will soon appear

July 6th

This is the day I came to Nigeria for better,
And not for worse
A family decision that was a blessing,
And not a curse
Today marks six adventurous years
Today I remember all the memories
The joys, successes, and tears

Never will you find a place like Nigeria
A one of a kind, a one in a million area
Just stay here for a week and you'll have stories to tell
About the house helps,
Mami show-shows,
And the reckless drivers as well

A country like this teaches you necessary skills
I've got tough skin, discernment, and religious zeal
At first I wasn't sure of this move,
And my head still lived in the States
But now I'm happy,
And know that this move was no mistake

Parents, thank you for bringing me here
Cheers to the special day in that year
The day I was exposed to my part of the world
July 6th, 2012 was the day,
That I became a very lucky girl

Context:

'House helps' is the Nigerian term for maids. In Nigeria, some of the stories about house helps are funny while others are a bit shocking. 'Mami show-shows' is a term used to describe women who are over-the-top. You can find them everywhere: school, work or church.

About the Poet and Author

Jemimah M. N. Ngu is a seventeen-year-old British-born Cameroonian poet, blogger (www.voxofjem.com) and student. She has had a talent for writing poetry from a very young age and has decided to share her work in *A Passage of Time*. This is her first collection of poems and she hopes to publish more.

Printed in Great Britain
by Amazon